Best wishes
from
Clive James

by the same author

THE METROPOLITAN CRITIC *Criticism* (*Faber & Faber*)

Collections of lyrics set and sung by Pete Atkin on the RCA label

BEWARE OF THE BEAUTIFUL STRANGER

DRIVING THROUGH MYTHICAL AMERICA

A KING AT NIGHTFALL

THE ROAD OF SILK

SECRET DRINKER

THE RIDER TO THE WORLD'S END

LIVE LIBEL

Song-book (*written with Pete Atkin*) (*Warner Bros. Music Ltd*)

A FIRST FOLIO

The FATE of FELICITY FARK in the LAND of the MEDIA

A Moral Poem
in Rhyming Couplets
by

CLIVE JAMES

With illustrations by
MARC

JONATHAN CAPE
THIRTY BEDFORD SQUARE LONDON

The Fate of Felicity Fark in the Land of the Media was first recited at the Institute of Contemporary Arts on the night of June 16th, 1975, under the auspices of the Poetry International Festival. The author narrated and Russell Davies supplied all the other voices.

FIRST PUBLISHED 1975
REPRINTED 1975

JONATHAN CAPE LTD, 30 BEDFORD SQUARE,
LONDON WC1

ISBN 0 224 01185 5

SET IN 12PT OLD STYLE 2PT LEADED

PRINTED PHOTOLITHO IN GREAT BRITAIN BY
EBENEZER BAYLIS & SON LTD
THE TRINITY PRESS, WORCESTER, AND LONDON

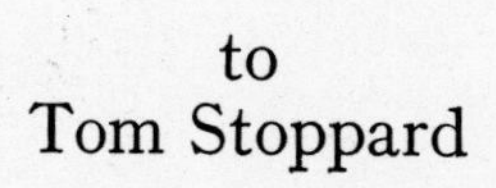
to
Tom Stoppard

MR HILARY. You talk like a Rosicrucian, who will love nothing but a sylph, who does not believe in the existence of a sylph, and who yet quarrels with the whole universe for not containing a sylph.

—Thomas Love Peacock, *Nightmare Abbey*

A GUIDE TO THE CHARACTERS OF THE LAND OF THE MEDIA

FELICITY FARK, an Innocent.
CAROL CLUNT, her mother: an artiste.
RAYMOND FARK, her father: a film director and vagrant.
MICHAEL LAPSE and DAVID VILE, two B.B.C. commentators.
KATIE WART, a beautiful chatelaine.
STUART GALL and WEARING EDDIE, two more B.B.C. commentators.
HARRY SEASLUG, a rotund tenor.
JESS FFOLKES, host of *Sunday Stars*: a man of God.
ARCHIE CANT (real name Michael Ramsey), variety artist and Primate of All England.
FRANK PAKAMAC, LORD FRUITCAKE, a humble Peer.
FREESIA, his daughter: a biographer.
HUGHIE CREEP, host of *This Is Your Break*.
SIR HUMPHREY HIGHRISE, a developer.
STANLEY STORKINS, a Northern playwright.
LORD POLAROID ('Larry'), tragedian and camera salesman.
CHIEF CLERK, an aesthete.
HAROLD HYPE, drama critic of the *Sunday Times*.
DAVID DROSS, a television personality.
PATRICK LOON, a crazed astronomer.
GREER GARSTLEIGH, an Australian feminist.
MICHAEL LIKEABLE and RUSSELL HUSTLE, two television interviewers.
HUGE WELSHMAN, B.B.C. Director-General and stand-up comic.
DICK JIGGLE, leader of the Bleeding Gits: a pop idol.

RUSS KENNEL, a controversial film-director.
BERNARD BEAVER, a music-loving journalist.
LORD TEDDYBEAR, the Poet Laureate.
LORD ARNOLD FATMAN, a sage.
PETER BERK, a controversial man of the theatre.
PETER BALLS, another controversial man of the theatre.
DOCTOR FRINGE ('Jonathan'), a prodigy.
ALAN WHANKER, a globe-trotting investigator.
PAULINE PLANK, a member of the public.
BRUCE HORSTEETH and BOB SKUNKHOUSE, two hosts of television quiz-shows.
MARY QUIM, a dressmaker.
YURI SPURI, a mountebank.
JOLLY MOLLY and JILLY SILLY, two fashionable scribblers.
ERIC MORE and ERNIE LESS, a comedy duo.
JELLY-ROLL BELLY ('Jelly'), jazz-singer and television-personality.
HAROLD HALF-PINT, an elliptical playwright.
LORD BUTCHFIELD, photographer and motorcyclist.
ANDRÉ PREVALENT, a boy musician.
SIR GEOFFREY RIPOFF, Minister of the Environment.
SIR BASIL SPENDTHRIFT, a speculative builder.
MARVIN GRABB and BUMPHREY QUARIUS, two cultural moderators.
KEN ONAN, sometime critic: a libertine.

AND

Errol Flynn, The Dame of Sark, General Custer, Jimmy Hill, Brian Clough, Basil Brush, Jack Jones, A. J. Ayer, Muhammad Ali, Dave Allen, Ken Dodd, Cary Grant, The Dalai Lama, Margot Fonteyn, John Logie Baird, Hermann Goering, John Keats, Charles Manson, Berthold Brecht, Henrik Ibsen, George Bernard Shaw, J. M. Barrie, Emile Zola, Emperor Hirohito, Mrs Patrick Campbell,

Sarah Bernhardt, Georges Braque, Princess Anne, Jean Renoir, Jack Nicklaus, Tiny Tim, Charlton Heston, Elizabeth Taylor, Richard Burton, Princess Grace, Maria Callas, Aristotle Onassis, Billie Jean King, Rod Laver, Glenda Jackson, Luis Bunuel, Federico Fellini, Wolfgang Amadeus Mozart, Marc Bolan, Ethel Merman, Martin Bormann, Clark Kent, Daniel Defoe, Jonathan Swift, Beau Brummel, Benjamin Disraeli, Kiri te Kanawa, Tommy Steele, John Conteh, Cliff Richard, Ronald Biggs, Billy Fury, Gary Glitter, Bernard Berenson, Peregrine Prykke, Anna Pest, George Best, David Hockney, Neville Chamberlain, William Shakespeare, Plato, Leonardo da Vinci, Diana Rigg, Karl Lagerfeld, Charles Conder, Shane Gould, Mark Spitz and many more.

BOOK ONE

OF erstwhile glories and the coming dark
I sing, and of the Innocent, FLICK FARK.
Of *Flick*—a name contracted from *Felicity*—
Who energized our Age like electricity
And finally, like nuclei in fission,
Sublimely altered out of recognition.
Lament! The Sweetling of Her Time is fled!
The fair name *Fark* no more on that fair head!
The girl we loved, sucked upward by osmosis,
Is lost inside her own Apotheosis!
But more of that stuff later. First, her Birth—
And straight away I must bemoan my dearth
Of skill to make the circumstances vivid
In which the babe was joyfully delivered.
It's not that ecstasy was on the cards.
The marriage was in fragments, ruins, shards—
In fact the bond had never reached the church,
Flick's mother having been left in the lurch
By RAYMOND FARK, a hack Yank movie-maker
Whose lust made *Errol Flynn* look like a Quaker.
The scene was *London*, 1948:
Just passing through, unfurnished with a date,
He lurched off to the *Windmill* on his tod,
Saw *Flick*'s mum in the chorus, mentioned *God*,
Impressed her with his silk sheets at the *Ritz*
And whispered words of love:
'Ya got *great* tits.'
She stayed a month, but then *Ray* had to go,
And back went CAROL CLUNT to *Pimlico*,
A stripper from the great days of her Art
When stately nudes who moved the aesthete's heart
Moved nothing of their own, but froze bare-breasted,
And if they scratched an itch they got arrested.

An honest trade—now lost, alas, to *Carol*,
A girl across (and looking like) a barrel,
Who met the day of her Confinement sadly:
No way could things turn out, it seemed, but badly.
With *England* short of everything but gloom,
The strained cries from that lonely basement room
Below a pastry shop behind *Victoria*
Could offer little prospect of euphoria—
And yet, when it, when *she* ... sheer revelation!
She lay there, cutest thing in all Creation!
A bagatelle who bleated like a lamb,
The birth-blood on her scalp like raspberry jam,
The cradle-cap like flakes of candied honey,
And, larger than half-crowns in the old money,
A pair of eyes you shivered to come near—
As blue and cloudless as the Stratosphere.
Let's say it was of joy that *Carol* died,
Transported by the Vision at her side:
And lest you mock so casual a fatality
Do please recall my purpose is Morality.
'I name my child *Felicity*,'

she said,

And well-contented she rolled over dead,
But then rolled back to add a codicil:
'And make it *Fark*, not *Clunt*,'

and so lay still.

Her final, and not smallest, claim to fame
Was thus to give her girl a magic Name,
A neat mnemonic whose alliteration
Would aid the kid in conquering the Nation,
And speed the day when *Pimlico*'s *Flick Fark*
Meant *London* like the *Dame* of *Sark* meant *Sark*.
At this point almost twenty years of time
Are cut away and tied off with a rhyme:
The tender tale's beyond my brittle Muse
Of how *Flick* climbed her ladder of new shoes—
Beginning in the grim Age of Austerity—
Towards the heady Era of Prosperity;
Of how the neighbours all mucked in and mothered her

And hugged the mite until they nearly smothered her;
Of how that doting district raised her up
As if they lifted the *Lycergus Cup*.
Had time allowed, it must have been my duty
To outline how she burgeoned into Beauty,
And grew from being merely twice as pretty
As any tot in that part of the city
To utter loveliness beyond comparison—
Unchallenged as the sword's-edge of the *Saracen*.
Time didn't, though, so why not cut the cackle?
Let's haul the plot along by block and tackle
Abruptly to the moment when *Flick Fark*,
As yet unknown, light-hearted as a lark,
Was working in a *chic King's Road* boutique
Whose catchy name was *Granny Takes a Leak*—
An airless cardboard kiosk flogging minis
At half a yard of cloth for fifty guineas.
One *Saturday* at noon, to get some air,
She popped out—and the world flamed like a flare
As purposeful technicians swarmed in hordes
With *Sun-guns*, floodlights and reflector boards.
A disembodied throat cried:

'Scrub the noise!
Turn over, camera. O.K., cue the boys,'
And two black ties, each topped off with a smile,
Bore down on her: MIKE LAPSE and DAVID VILE!
'And here she is, the girl they all call *Flick*,'
Exulted *Vile*,

'the girl they could well pick
From alla *London*'s bride young things to hold
The tidal of "*Miss Knockout*"!'

Then the bold
Yet well-brushed tones of *Lapse* took up the theme:
'*Felicity*, perhaps today your dream
Comes true. Of all the girls left in the running
You are the least affected and most stunning.
Our judges have been cruising around town
In secret now for weeks. They've whittled down
A great long list to you, you gorgeous thing.

But first, some tricky questions. Can you sing?'
'I'm sorry, Mr *Lapse*,'
sighed *Flick*,
'but no.'
Said *Lapse*:
'Then can you dance, embroider, sew?
Does music take your interest? Pictures? Books?
Is all you've got to give the world your looks?'
'I'm sorry,'
stammered *Flick*,
'but that's the truth.'
'I name you, then, "*Miss Knockout*"—Queen of Youth!'
Cried *Lapse*, at which point judges from all nations
Arranged on rostra roared congratulations
While hoisting skyward an unbroken line
Of coloured score-cards all marked 9.9.
The cheering *Chelsea* dwellers choked *King's Road*:
They swelled and surged and raged and ebbed and
flowed,
Until—a great *Cunarder* from its jetty
Superbly trailing streamers and confetti—
The stately KATIE WART ploughed through, to set
Upon *Flick*'s head a diamond coronet,
So brilliant on its cushion of mock mink
It well-nigh fused the *Eurovision Link*.
'And there she is, she's crowned at last,'
Vile stressed,
'The girl who, whom, that, no one could of guessed
Would one day be—this unknown orphan girl
Who grew up lonely like a ... like a pearl,
This girl they call the Pearl of *Pimlico*—
Would be the "*Knockout*" Score-Girl! Now we know.'
Like *General Custer Flick Fark* was surrounded:
She stood her ground less steadfast than astounded,
And might have turned to flee had not the matey
Mature and motherly support of *Katie*
Been radiating comfort at her shoulder—
As warm as toast, yet solid as a boulder.

'*Es ist,*'

chirped *Katie,*

'*ein* great *jour*, my dear,

And *molto gloire* lies in your *avvenir*.'

For *Katie* spoke a *Euro-Esperanto*

Which sounded like a souped-up *Pisan canto.*

In *Stockport, Stockholm, Split* and *Salamanca*

The viewers loved her fluent lingua franca.

Relaxed and regal, poised and polyglot

La Wart knew *chi* was who and *quoi* was what.

From cuticle to coiffe, from skin to core,

She could have outclassed Madame *Pompadour*

And made *Récamier* or *Montespan*

Seem something tasteless served up from a can.

The Age of Gold saw nothing like such grooming:

She would have left those Frog slags fairly *fuming.*

A head-and-shoulder shot zoomed tight on *Flick.*

The titles rolled. The monitors went click.

'*Finito*!'

carolled *Katie,*

'*Dass* was fun.

Ma voiture is close by. *Wir müssen* run.

You've got *un altro* job to do today.

Tu peux changer your schmutter on the way.'

BOOK TWO

THEY climbed into a drop-head *Park Ward Bentley*
Which *Wart* seemed indisposed to handle gently.
She steamed along at seldom less than eighty
(Waved on by policemen calling
'Hello Katie!')
While *Flick* made shift to don some type of track-suit—
A sort of spray-on rayon *Union Jack*-suit.
Through zebra-crossing, roundabout and stoplight
Wart carved a bloody pathway like a hoplite,
Yet never did the fury of her charge
So much as dent her famous *maquillage*,
Which glittered as if forged from chrome-vanadium
When through the gateway of a looming stadium
They sped to find a numberless assembly
Of shrieking '*Knockout*' fans.
'And here at *Wembley*
It's *Britain* versus *Europe*. Can we do it?
We can!'
cried STUART GALL,
'So let's go to it!
And here's a lass who no one's seen before
To lend us heart by helping to keep score!
Where *France* had *Helen*, *Troy* had *Joan* of *Arc*,
Great Britain's '*Knockout*' Squad have got *Flick Fark*!'
As *Flick* was led away to man the score-board—
An all-decked-out-with-flashing-lights-galore-board—
The gun went off. The first game was beginning!
And straight away the *Germans* started winning.
Down giant slides made slick with mud they slipped
And in their fists great swords and shields they gripped.
Like *Heinkel* pilots through the air they flew
And flocks of vampire bats they bravely slew,
Before, like bombs, they plunged into a brimming

Aquarium stocked full of slowly swimming
Electric rays and hungry crocodiles—
And always their square heads were wreathed in smiles,
While *Stuart* bellowed:

'Yes, *Great Britain*, yes!
You *must* win this or else we're in a mess!
Oh yes! Oh YES! Oh no! Oh dear! Oh Hell.
We really should have won that one. Oh well,
These *Krauts* are all pro athletes in disguise—
And anyway, the sun was in our eyes.'
The *Jerries* scored full marks in every game.
Their total soared, the *U.K.*'s stayed the same.
The sole thing *Flick* could do to aid our heroes
Was grin a plucky grin and mark up zeroes.
And yet, against all odds, she felt fulfilled:
Her blithe young being weirdly throbbed and thrilled.
She strangely became more and more elated
The more the home team's hopes became deflated.
As *Britain* trailed the *Swedes* and then the *Swiss*
She first knew perfect pleasure, then sheer bliss.
But wait! For *Britain*'s chance was not yet gone.
There yet remained the *Mini-Marathon*,
In which the fattest man from each contingent
Was handcuffed in a manner firm and stringent
And hung up blindfold from a high trapeze.
Attached to it by nothing but his knees,
He dodged hot custard pies above a pit
Containing fifty tons of steaming ...

'It
Ah looks, ee-ooh, like our-ah, ooh-ee, chap
Might ooh, just keep, ee-ah, out of the crap,'
Laughed *B.B.C.* reporter WEARING EDDIE,
With diction lucid as his stance was steady.
''E's swervin' well, e's ooh, as keen as mustard.
A brave lad, this. 'Is 'ed is *drippin'* custard.'
But then the boy dropped out of the event
And disappeared into the excrement.
With voice cacophonous and manners callous
The *German* fans sang "*Deutschland über alles*"

And clapped hands as their team marched off upon a
Mechanically delighted lap of honour,
At which the beaten *British* crew, poor wretches,
Were bandaged up and bundled on to stretchers
While *Stuart, Eddie, Lapse* and *Vile, Frank Bough,*
Don Revie, Jimmy Hill and *Brian Clough*
Discussed, downcast, the *U.K.*'s lack of flair
With *Basil Brush, Jack Jones* and *A. J. Ayer.*

The heart of *Flick Fark*, on the other hand,
Was high, and thumping fit to beat the band.
Throughout the match she'd felt as if caressed
By ghostly fingertips touched to her breast
Which traced with practised ease a killing ripple
Of little chills around each aching nipple.
Another bunch of fairy digits based
Their efforts on the sweet skin round her waist,
While yet another searched between her thighs
In ways that filled her eyes with wild surmise.
Inducing groans that bordered on satiety
The phantom force groped onward like a deity
Priapic as those Gods who hotly hovered
Above the clueless heroines of *Ovid*:
Its mitts were many as the Empress *Kali*'s
And travelled faster than *Muhammad Ali*'s.
It was the Lens that stroked her and unloosed her:
The Camera was the satyr that seduced her.
It was the Cathode Tube that laved her features
As wet tongues lick the fuzz from skins of peaches.
The insubstantial swain was Electronic
Who made *Flick*'s haemoglobin fizz like tonic.
A lover both importunate and prurient
As well as inexhaustibly esurient,
The suitor for *Flick*'s favours was THE MEDIA—
Who, greedy now, would soon be even greedier.
The Virgin had consumed the Magic Potion:
Her metamorphosis was now in motion.
Already she'd half left the mortal scrimmage
And part-way started to become an *Image*.
Small wonder that the fair face of *Flick Fark*
Seemed made of light alone, a living spark,
As half a hundred million *British* viewers
Who hadn't seen a thing they liked since *Suez*
Sat clucking with unbounded satisfaction
At *Flick*'s undoubted powers of attraction,
While like an avalanche or even faster
Their '*Knockout*' Squad went screaming to disaster.

'*Ma chère*, you were *sehr hübsch*,'

cried *Katie Wart*,

'*Mais* now you must outgrow *die Welt* of Sport.
Tomorrow *notte* you're on "*Sunday Stars*".
Vamos a casa mia to change cars.
We'll drive to *Leeds und da* rehearse your Dance.
Allons-y, cara. Snap *aus* of your trance.'
And once again the maid *Flick Fark* fared forth—
And through the falling night rode to the North.

BOOK THREE

I SWEAR that '*Sunday Stars*' was, at this time,
As close as TV gets to the Sublime.
Its cast of Showbiz Big Names gave the Nation
A whole new Sacrament—COMMUNICATION.
When HARRY SEASLUG sang
'*I'll Waltz With God*'
God rated like *Dave Allen* or *Ken Dodd*.
The Format gave the *Gospels* Credibility
And *Christ* the thing he needed most—Virility.
It lent the *Holy Ghost* a new Humanity
And put Charisma into *Christianity*.
The show's M.C. was that most blest of blokes—
Your friend and mine, *God*'s right-hand man,
JESS FFOLKES.
Of opalescent cheek and bubble forehead
In which a holy radiance flared florid,
Jess Ffolkes's face was puckered at the lips
To drink the Sacred Word in tiny sips
While smiling as though stricken by the *Gorgon*
Perpetually behind his trembling Organ.
Some saw in the façade of *Jess*'s cranium
A poppy pushed into a pink geranium.
We married men were mostly put in mind
Of underneath a baby girl's behind,
While others found—I think this somewhat coarse—
The aft of an albino *Arab* horse.
'Well, here we are again to praise Our *Lord*,'
Said *Jess*, and from his Organ dripped a chord,
'And here's a lovely letter I've been sent
By *Pauline Plank* of *Cretinthorpe* in *Kent*.
It says: "Dear Mr *Ffolkes*, do please convey
My thanks to *God* in your distinguished way
For watching over me. The house next door

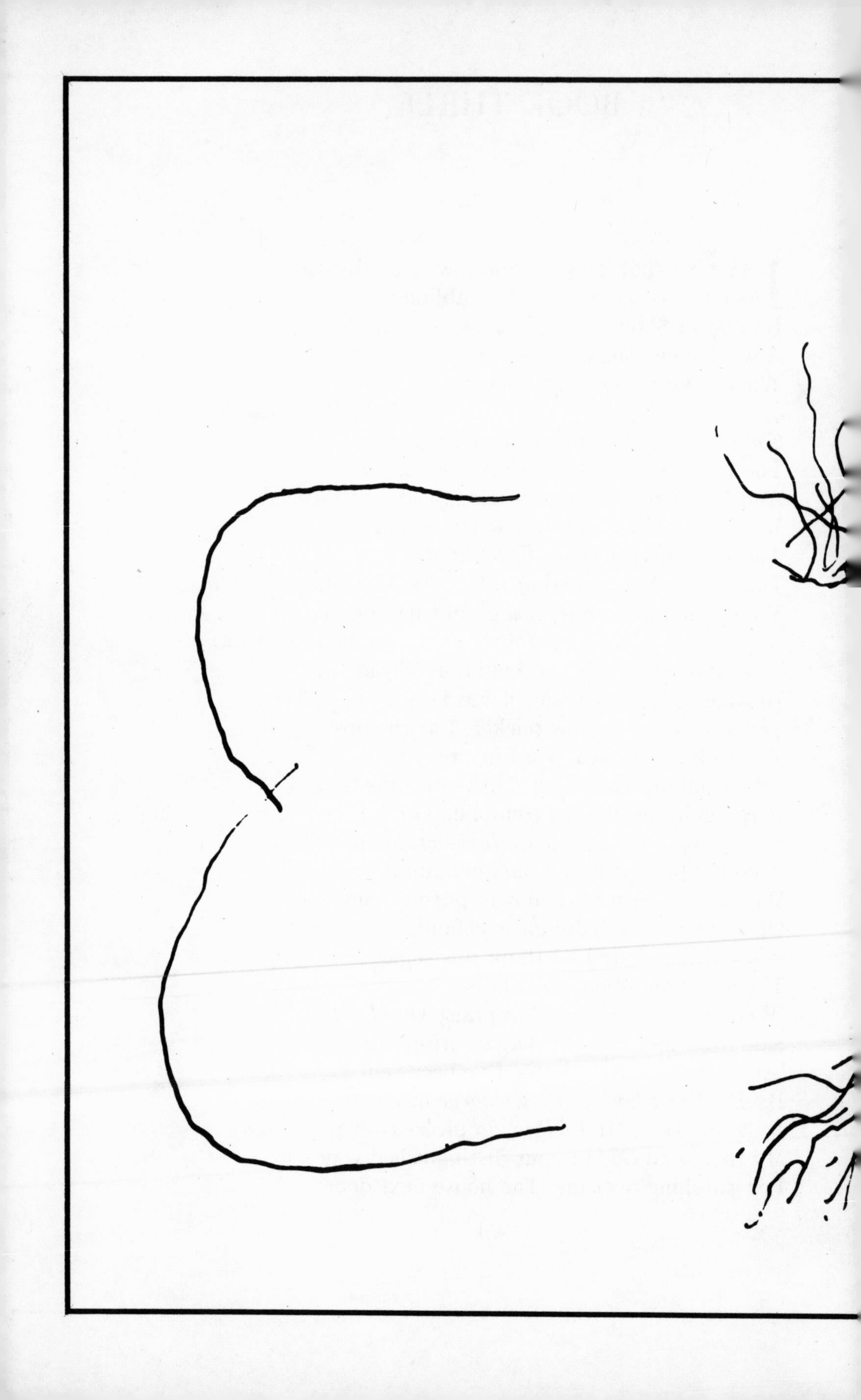

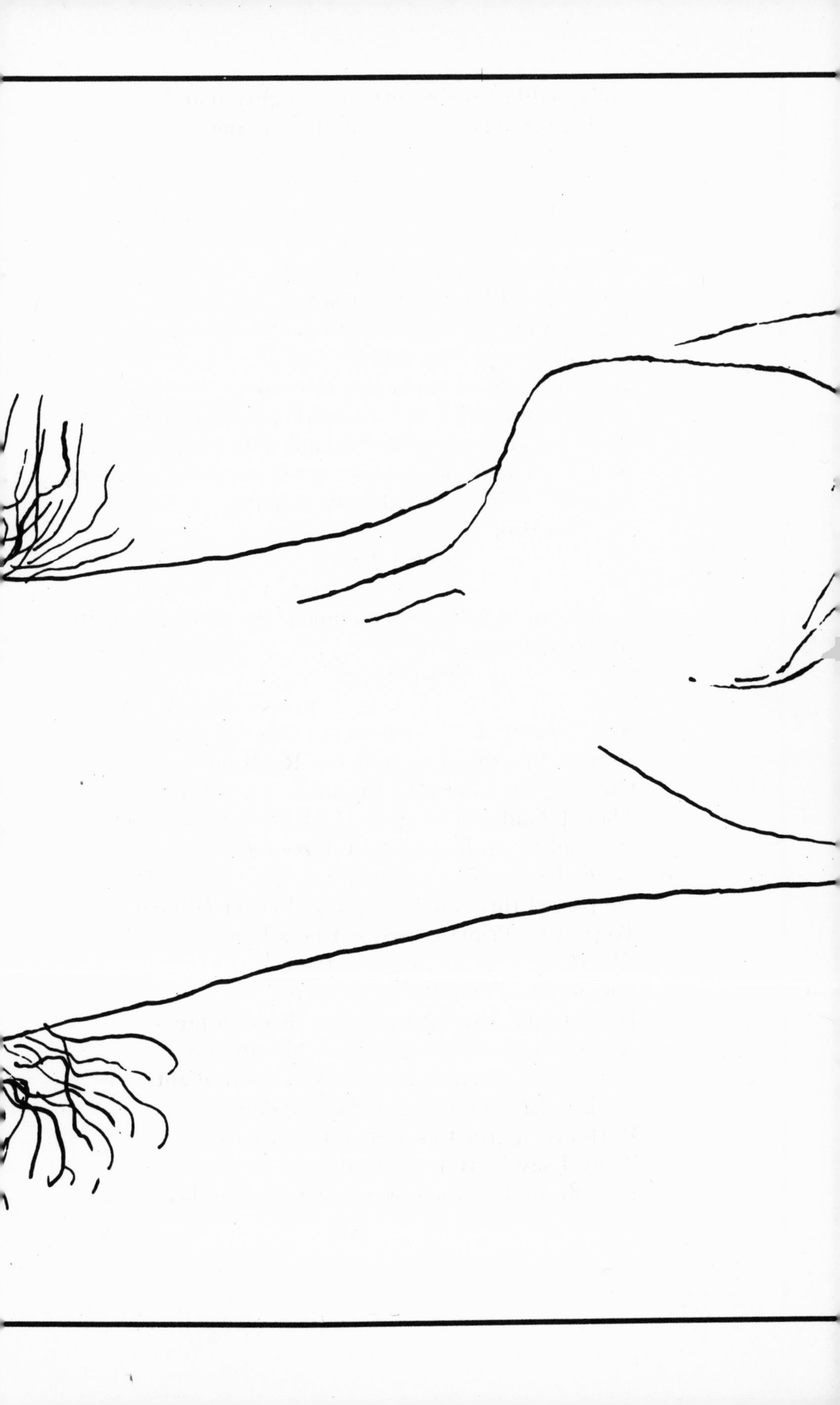

Pull-out of the Year

"From *Zion*'s daughter beauty is departed," '
Sang *Archie Cant*, but, far from broken-hearted,
Seemed thrilled by every sentence of his text.
He cycled off, while *Jess Ffolkes* simpered:
'Next
We give you that extremely pious Peer—
The Paragon permissive people fear—
That neo-*Nazarene* of the Nobility,
FRANK PAKAMAC, LORD FRUITCAKE, on Humility.'
From where *Flick Fark* stood waiting to go on
Lord Fruitcake's skull seemed polished till it shone.
His skin looked famished as the *Hindu Kush*
Yet blazed with splendour like the Burning Bush.
The hardest-bitten Cynic's heart would crumble
To gaze upon a countenance so Humble.
It seemed to *Flick* that this man *hated* Fame:
He scorned it as *St Lawrence* scorned the flame.
A sad *St Catherine* broken on the Wheel,
With diffidence he launched into his Spiel.
It rolled before his eyes on *Autocue*
And yet he made it all sound new and true.
'For me—I think I have to say "for me"
(I say "I think", of course, advisedly)—
Humility is what my poor soul craves.
I think it's what was meant by *Jesus* Saves.
Myself, I think that I—and I say "I" ...'
And so he nattered on, and by and by
The subject of his piece became Pornography.
His daughter *Freesia* deals in Biography.
Of every age and epoch, creed and party,
She hymns the salient illuminati:
Though more than all those Lives (the thought occurs)
The Life most stuffed with incident is *hers*,
Whose binding remains singularly fine
Considering the pressure on the spine.
Lord Fruitcake's second daughter scribbles fiction.
His wife, too, shares the scrivening addiction.
Throughout the *Kingdom* inky quills are flailing:
The whole damned bloodline shares the Family Failing.

In all the lighter literary forms
The *Pakamacs* are on the job in swarms,
And just to sketch that dynasty's daft saga
Would swiftly drive me absolutely ga-ga—
So let's get back as quickly as we can
To concentrating on the clan's top man.
'I think of my Humility—and I
Am conscious, naturally, that saying "my"
Obliges me—and I say "me", of course ... '
But here his drone seemed somehow drained of force,
For even as he savoured his own prose
The beady orbs on each side of his nose
Distractedly were focusing in common on
A gratifying optical phenomenon
Whose powers to enchant outstripped the pen's:
He saw his face reflected in the lens.
While everybody waited with breath bated
He stood there fascinated and fixated.
He imitated *Lot*'s Wife turned to salt
While all around the Show ground to a halt.
Subjecting his sweet self to stunned inspection—
A Humble witness at the *Resurrection*—
Lord Fruitcake looked as love-sick as *Narcissus*
In vain upon the water raining kisses.
As men in white coats led the poor oaf off
Jess Ffolkes's Organ gave a little cough.
Its master was quite used to these disasters
And suavely burbled on as if on casters.
'Tonight on "*Sunday Stars*" we have the pleasure
Of showing off a brand-new National Treasure.
Flick Fark, a lass as pure as she is pretty,
Will do a Dance to that majestic ditty
We cling to when all other Hope has flown—
The lovely hymn, "*You'll Never Walk Alone*".'
So saying, *Jess* manipulated knobs.
His trusty Organ heaved with sobs and throbs,
While eerily across the floor there hissed
Infinitudes of filmy, flimsy mist—
As fluffy-soft and faery-white as when

Those cloudy shrouds of liquid oxygen
Submerge the launch-pad in a cold lagoon
Before *Apollo* lifts off for the Moon.
You couldn't see for looking, look for seeing,
As through that Sea of Dreams *Flick Fark* came fleeing,
A footloose firefly like *Tinkerbell*—
Yet wispy as a *Willi* from 'Giselle'.
Her movements both unstudied and unfettered,
She pranced, she paused, she posed, she pirouetted—
Her poise *God*-given like the *Dalai Lama*'s—
In pastel turquoise Baby-Doll pyjamas.
Ingested at her local Comprehensive,
Flick's repertoire of steps was not extensive.
No critic of the Dance would, in *Flick Fark*,
See any threat to *Fonteyn* or *Merle Park*.
An infinitely sensual simplicity
Was all that you could credit to *Felicity*.
But it sufficed: a shy though sprightly doe,
She sprang from toe to light fantastic toe.
Egged on by *Jess*'s eager Implement
She seemed by wave upborne, by tradewind sent,
A figment of the blue *Aegean* day—
A sunlight ghost, a spectre in the spray.
She danced, and lo! Her minuscule chemise
Looked not much more substantial than a breeze.
With air puffed out and here and there sucked in
Her gauzy garb did great things for her skin.
To how and where that fragile fabric floated
The camera-eye unswervingly devoted
A penetrating, probing, sub-cutaneous
Regard that found all other views extraneous.
The Show's entire staff joined in the scrutiny.
The camera crews were on the verge of mutiny:
They twisted their controls as if convulsed.
And through it all *Jess Ffolkes*'s Organ pulsed—
It twitched and lurched towards a Major Crisis
As though it were attached to *Dionysus*.
And now the whole of *Britain* fell full length
For *Flick* with all its Heart and Soul and Strength.

And now the Faith which once made *Blighty* mighty
Was lavished on a nymphette in a nightie.
And now, as *Flick Fark*'s features filled the screen,
The spasms of *Jess Ffolkes*'s great Machine
Were surging with a turgid urge to merge
And mingle in one potent, purging splurge—
An overwhelming flood of sonic spume
That swept *Flick* off into the dressing-room.
'*Cherie, es war ein cosa fantastique*:
Je suis so froh che I can hardly speak!'
Cried *Katie* as *Flick* fell into her arms,
Thus calming the poor darling's fears and qualms.
For *Flick* was ironed flat by her endeavour:
She thought that she could go to sleep forever.
She lolled like a Slow Loris on *Largactil*
And felt as wiped out as the *Pterodactyl*.
Tremendous as a tantrum from the *Führer*
La Wart's barbaric *Lamborghini Miura*
Went belting through the dark down the *M1*
At many miles per hour above the Ton.
As *Katie* drove (and what uncanny grace
The dashboard glow conferred upon her face!)
She prattled about all the marvellous things
That *Flick* would find were waiting in the wings.
And through *Flick*'s drowsy mind the Future flowed,
And all along that magic midnight road
The to-ing tail-lights and the fro-ing headlights
Seemed not just large white lights and little red lights
But stones so precious Kings could not afford them.
Great pearls in golden cobwebs flew toward them.
A cataract of rubies raged ahead.
While *Flick*, fagged out, lay back as though in bed
And closed her eyes against the hail of jewels,
Her coach of glass, propelled by precious fuels,
Ran Southward like a clap of rolling thunder
To seek the City lying ripe for plunder.

BOOK FOUR

By rough arithmetic it seems I've penned
Three books of verse describing one weekend.
At that rate, if I've moved the proper decimal,
The *Iliad* will look infinitesimal
When judged for length beside my finished libel,
Which could outweigh both *Beowulf* and the *Bible*
Combined with *Dante*, *Virgil* and *Lucretius*—
But harping on this theme would sound facetious.
Be brief! To speed your couplets through the weeks
And catch the Vital Moment when it speaks!
To strip the silent seasons from the year
And seize the day advancing *Flick*'s career!
Let *Aprils* bloom, leave brown *Novembers* burning,
And leap through Time to watch the Decade turning!
For only swift and pitiless elision
Can sum up *Flick*'s Success on Television.
Our sweetheart was a fixture on the Box
The way *Andromeda* was on the rocks:
She was, without a whisper of dissension,
The captive Queen of *Logie Baird*'s invention.
By morning, noon and night and all next day
She creamed herself with lather of *Camay*,
While voices on the sound-track called it
'larther'—
A savoury burst of fragrant adman's blarther.
She primped herself with This, she preened with That,
She fed ten tons of protein to the Cat:
She chose a tube of These instead of Those
And confidently crammed them up her nose.
She said that
'Beanz Meanz *Heinz*!'
and
'*Heinz* Meanz Beanz!'

And added

'*Flash* Potato Really Cleanz!'

She claimed

'*Daz* Cooks My Undies Baby-White!'

And

'*Ajax* Shines My Baby *Ultrabrite*!'

She warned against the dreaded *Understains*
And showed how *Dynorods* did out her drains.
And so, in scads (nay, myriads) of ads
She flogged the fads to doting mums and dads—
Which meant she almost never left the screen,
Since she was also in the shows between.
BRUCE HORSTEETH and BOB SKUNKHOUSE both used *Flick*
To help contestants sort out what to pick
From pyramids of garbage in all guises
They had the hide to give away as prizes.
For HUGHIE CREEP, *Flick* jumped out of a cake
And told the winner on

'*This Is Your Break*'

How glad she was to see him/her/them win,
Kissed him/her/them, and deftly jumped back in.
In short, on telly *Flick* was so ubiquitous
Her omnipresence seemed almost iniquitous:
She tended at that stage, although adorable,
To strike the higher-minded as deplorable.
But *Pimlico* saw stature in its pin-up:
Flick was the girl who helped it keep its chin up.
The place had lost that Safe-as-Houses feeling:
The Boom in Property had set it reeling.
The trumpets for the Dance of Death were blowing
And ancient Ways of Life were quickly going—
Since every blessed thing not to their taste
DEVELOPERS were swiftly laying waste.
At negligible risk, with aim unerring,
They pulverized more real estate than *Goering*,
And on each dwelling's ruin raised a Tower—
To Maximize a Prime Site's Earning-Power.
Of all *God*'s greedy creatures on two legs

Developers must surely be the dregs.
The cut-throats even cause LORD TEDDYBEAR,
Our child-like *Laureate*, to tear his hair.
These were the Get Rich Quick years of a gang
Who should, by rights, have been condemned to hang,
Or else to burn, or—no, not or: and—freeze.
Instead, the bastards all got *K.B.E.*s.
A vandal who, by general estimation,
Outdid them all in total devastation
And knocked down swathes of *London* just for fun,
SIR HUMPHREY HIGHRISE was their Number One.
His Aspect was Unknown: he Shunned Society.
His Name, however, dripped with notoriety.
In *Pimlico* his hoardings filled the skies:

THIS TOWER IS A *HIGHRISE* ENTERPRISE.
10,000 TOP-CLASS OFFICES TO LET,
COMPRISING A FINE PENTHOUSE-MAISONETTE
WITH PANORAMIC OUTLOOK ON *BULGARIA*.
A *HIGHRISE* CONTRIBUTION TO YOUR AREA.

Such castles stood cold shoulder to cold shoulder
And in between fell shadows even colder.
The Mews where *Flick* was born, though, still survived,
And there she stayed no matter how she thrived,
Her basement room below the pastry shop
Persisting as if Time had had a Stop.
And still the local swains were sick with longing,
Though now a more exotic breed came thronging
To take her to the places and the parties
Where people ate Amphetamines like *Smarties*
And coughed their callow lives away like *Keats*—
The other *London* underneath the streets.
She stunned a crowded room like the *Medusa*
When lunching at *Trattoo* or *Arethusa*.
Among the languid diners at *Chez Victor*
She lounged about as if a mule had kicked her.

Her pubic hair designed by *Mary Quim,*
She danced (in army boots from *Hung Like Him*)
The whole night long at *Annabel*'s or *Tramp*—
A naiad of the darkly rising damp.
Eurydice was in the Underworld—
But let me hear no sniff, see no lip curled:
I grant *Flick* lived the Life-Style of the Young
In ecstasies that verged on the unstrung,
But still must hasten here to treat dismissively
Contentions that she led that life *Permissively*.

Far from it. The unfashionable fact
Was this: the *Golden Girl remained intact.*
Her attitudes may not have *looked* strait-laced,
But underneath it all, *Flick Fark* was Chaste.
Our Heroine repressed all thoughts of Sex
The way the *Russian* army crushed the *Czechs.*
Tenaciously retaining her good humour
At how the gossip columns seethed with rumour
And linked her name with everybody eligible
In dithyrambs both trite and unintelligible,
She held herself in patient readiness
For Holy Matrimony, nothing less.
I don't suggest our Darling was a schemer:
I simply mean she dreamed of a Redeemer.
She conjured up some clean-cut *Galahad*
Whom Fate decreed should be the lucky lad:
She saw a scene where *Lohengrin* came on
In shining armour standing on a swan
And clamorously sprang ashore to settle
Her doubts in his embrace of heavy metal.
Assessing pros and cons there'd be no call for:
She knew her Heart would tell her who to fall for.
But though the girl had strength, her name lacked weight
And then one night the phone rang, very late.
'Ah, *da* you are, you *kleine* gadabout!
How strange *trouver* you in, instead of out.'
The earpiece squawked in tones of fond reproof—
Which were, *Flick* feared, a teensy bit aloof.
'You've earned some cash, but *jetzt* you need *cachet.*
Je pense it's time you did *ein* West End play.
Report *domani* at *le Royal Court.*
Bonne nuit, tesoro. Ciao!'
quacked *Katie Wart.*
The Northern Playwright STANLEY STORKINS greeted
Our favourite while remaining firmly seated.
Before them stretched the empty auditorium
As plush as a *Victorian* emporium.

Stan Storkins looked as North as you can get
Before the land runs out and you get wet;
As Northern as the boatswain of a lugger
In difficulties North of *Muckle Flugga*;
As Northern as the grave of *Fridtjof Nansen*—
With pointed spiral eyeballs like *Charles Manson.*
'The play,'
said *Storkins,*
'is called "*Roll on Death*".
Were you at RADA?'
Here *Flick* caught her breath.
'I'm sorry,'
twittered *Flick,*
'I've had no training.'
'Don't worry, love. You won't find *me* complaining.
With "*Roll on Death*" I probe my deep anxieties
And correlate *my* anguish with Society's
In Confrontations which, though not simplistic,
Are always resolutely Realistic.
No play I've written's caused me so much grief:
The way I've spilled my guts defies belief.'
Thus *Storkins* spake, and thus he spake much more,
And more and more *Flick Fark* was numb with awe.
In plays by *Stanley Storkins*, she now learned,
The genius of *Bertolt Brecht* returned.
Compared with *Storkins, Ibsen, Shaw* and *Jarry*
Were bourgeois liberal hacks like *J. M. Barrie.*
The Western World, to this updated *Zola,*
Was just a molar soaked in *Coca-Cola.*
'You might call "*Roll on Death*" a post-*Hegelian*
Uncompromising Version of "*Pygmalion*"—
A Social Structure flayed to the last layer
In which *you* play a naked *Galatea.*'
Disturbed at this, *Flick* still was overjoyed:
Her leading man would be LORD POLAROID!
Lord Polaroid, the show-piece of the Peerage,
Has never been inclined to travel Steerage.
He's always been a thespian Equestrian
Who looks on walking as a bit pedestrian.

Unbending as befits a veteran Titan,
He dwells in the *Pavilion* down at *Brighton.*
Most rarely is he tempted up to town,
But when he is, he puts on robes and crown
And rides in his own train, the *Brighton Belle*—
The rails are laid direct to his hotel.
For *Polaroid* to play in *Stan*'s confection
Was not, however, *that* strange a connection:
For years the Peer had maintained his ascendancy
By clambering aboard the latest tendency—
Though truth to tell he'd signed for '*Roll on Death*'
Believing he'd been asked to do '*Macbeth*'.
The Noble made his entry incognito,
As tentative as Emperor *Hirohito.*
Two gentlemen-in-waiting and one page
Sufficed to keep his robes clear of the stage.
In front of him a flunkey knelt and gripped
A calf-bound, gold-tooled copy of the script,
Through which the stern praetorian leafed pensively,
Blue-pencilling the minor parts extensively.
In time the pencil's point got blunt, then broke.
He looked at it, looked peeved, looked up, and spoke.
'My first line, here: I'd like to take that out
And put in something better. What about
"A horse, a horse, my something for a horse"?
Not that I want to interfere, of course.'
'I'm sure you're right,'
said *Storkins*.
'Now Miss *Fark*,
If you could take your clothes off, find your mark,
And sort of, you know, more or less just *stand*
(While doing kind of *this* with your left hand),
We'll block it from the top speech on page one.'
Their monumental labour had begun.

I can lick any girl in this bar.....

BOOK FIVE

FLICK staggered home each night limp with fatigue,
Exalted to be in the Major League.
She found the concentration of rehearsal
More challenging by far than plugging *Persil.*
She studied books on Theory of Theatre
To try and understand *Stan Storkins* better.
She found herself sought out by the Posh Press
And asked if she had set aside Success.
'I felt that it was high time to *commit* myself:
To pick up something angular and *hit* myself.
I needed to do something that would *stretch* me,
And that's when *Stan* and *Larry* came to fetch me.
I *love* them both, though not the way you've heard:
They're both grown men. I doubt the thought's
occurred.'
The frequency with which *Stan* would adjust
Flick's pose did not arise, she knew, from Lust.
The reason *Storkins* failed to keep his distance
Was simply his desire to give assistance.
The same with *Polaroid*, who helped her doff
Her dressing-gown each time she took it off—
And, when the moment came for her to don
That garment, raced to help her put it on.
And in this wise the calendar lost leaves
With many whisperings of subtle sleeves,
Until at last the time was up for certain.
Flick stood there in the buff behind the curtain
And felt it race away. She faced a blur
Of half-seen people. *They* saw *all* of *her*.
Their blasé expectations took a battering.
Good *God*, this girl was positively shattering!
The galaxy of eyes made *Flick* feel hot—
Conspicuous as *Jupiter*'s Red Spot.

That aggregate of well-heeled culture-vultures—
The usual desperadoes and drygulchers—
For once in their indulgent lives were hushed,
As *Flick*'s unsullied epidermis blushed.
CHIEF CLERK's great disquisition on '*The Nude*'
Must somewhere in its amplitude allude
To forms that matched *Flick Fark*'s in sheer sublimity.
But even he, for all his magnanimity,
That night would have pronounced her without equal—
A Beauty without harbinger or sequel.
She was a dream by *Boucher* or *Watteau*,
A raspberry ripple of the *Rococo*—
Yet also a *Madonna* by *Bellini*,
Or even *St Teresa* by *Bernini*.
A *Magdalene* by *Fra Filippo Lippi*
Beside *Flick*'s sweetness would have looked a cheapie:
She could have made the average *Botticelli*
Seem something published yearly by *Pirelli*.
But while I draw these parallels from painting,
Remember that the Audience was fainting.
They nodded as if strung out, stoned or sauced:
The Play worked like a motor-car's exhaust.
Though buoyed up by the vision of *Flick*'s nudity
They yawned aloud at *Stan*'s dramatic crudity.
It was a war of drugs, if you can picture it—
With *Flick* the benzedrine, *Stan* the barbiturate.
The Play, like all of *Stanley*'s dramaturgy,
Outpointed a convention of the Clergy
For rhetoric wrapped up in solemn twaddle.
Our darling was supposed to be a Model
Who posed for Students learning Art, poor creature—
With *Polaroid* obliged to play their teacher.
To summarize the plot would be invidious,
Except to say its tedium was hideous.
Though *Polaroid* beefed up each dreary speech
('The *King*'s to blame! Once more into the breach!'),
From *Stan* the English Language got no lift:
To load a rift with ore he lacked the gift.
He fumbled words and clumsily dispensed them

As if he held their elegance against them.
His every play a turkey frozen frigid,
In point of fact he bored the public rigid:
Their secret view of *Stanley*'s stuff was
'Shove it'.
The CRITICS, though, instructed them to love it.
The *London* Drama Critics worship thickness:
They view agility as simply slickness.
The *London* Drama Critics loathe the light touch:
They think a grizzly's clutch might be the right touch.
The *London* Drama Critics, as a species,
Detect the smell of frankincense in faeces.
The *London* Drama Critics give indemnity
To dunderheads who sanctify solemnity:
They tie the tag Contemporary Playwright
On dolts who couldn't get the time of day right.
They all were there to see *Flick* do her number:
They took notes while the audience fought slumber.
They all looked as anonymous as eels,
But one of them, *Flick* noticed, was on wheels.
His name was HAROLD HYPE. In perpetuity
Hype leads the holy war against acuity.
His judgment is unfailingly appalling:
He is, therefore, the Captain of his Calling.
For years *Hype* has adorned the *Sunday Times*
With stuff so overwrought it almost rhymes.
An oyster-shell and broken-glass mosaic,
In vain his prose strives not to be prosaic:
Secreting sugar like a diabetic
It well-nigh busts a gut to be poetic.
On *Stanley*'s Play at last the curtain fell
And everybody present ran pell-mell.
The fate of '*Roll on Death*', it seemed, was sealed:
No sign of life save *Flick* had it revealed.
But *Harold Hype* hummed home on spokes of chromium
Composing in his head a wild encomium:
He hurried to his desk on hubs of nickel,
So urgent was his treacle's need to trickle.
'One is both pleased and terrified,'
typed *Hype*

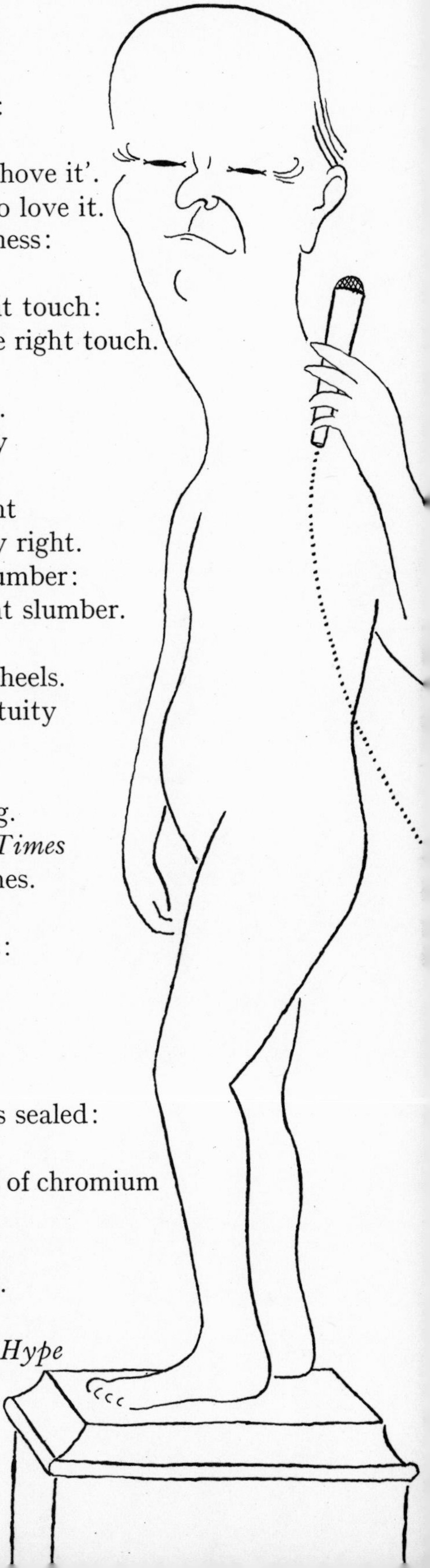

(And instantly you taste the tang of tripe)
'To see this playwright's magnitude increase.
His new work is a Blazing Masterpiece!
The silent *Royal Court* seemed consecrated:
Within its walls true greatness was created.
When dedicated men attain beatitude
What other answer can we give but gratitude?
Lord Polaroid's performance was a miracle ... '
(And here for several columns *Hype* waxed lyrical)
'It should, however, ringingly be said ... '
(For *Hype* assumed the things he said got read)
'That this play finds the fullness of its splendour
In one of a more tender age and gender:
I mean Miss *Fark*, who neither speaks nor stirs,
Yet permeates each action that occurs
With softer tendrils than the sea anemone—
As fraught with Fate as kisses in *Gethsemane*.
It may be perilous, but I shall gamble,
And call Miss *Fark* a Mrs *Patrick Campbell*.
Perhaps—nay, probably!—another *Sarah*.
I swear not even *Florence Farr* was fairer ... '
And so for ages *Hype* drooled on demented,
Besotted by the myth he had invented;
And when the piece appeared in print, *Flick Fark*
Was there on the same page with *Braque* and *Bach*;
Her picture, as it always did, raised eyebrows—
The eyebrows this time, though, belonged to highbrows.

BOOK SIX

So yet again with scalpel and with suture
We slice and stitch a short-cut to the future.
A year went by and still the Play was running,
And every night *Flick* stood there looking stunning.
The Glossy Magazines had gone bananas:
They went for her like *Anne* goes for gymkhanas.
In *Vogue* there was a brilliant two-page spread
Consisting of the top bit of *Flick*'s head:
And then the bottom bit came out in *Queen*—
And *Harper*'s ran the bit left in between.
She looked much more prestigious, if less pally,
Than when she'd posed for *Tit-Bits* and *Reveille*.
In better-class photographers, *Flick* learned,
The gem-like flame of Inspiration burned.
They weren't like those cheap pimps with dirty minds
And dark-rooms out the back with broken blinds
Who tried to get your bra off in the car:
Instead, they were True Artists like *Renoir*
Who owned converted monasteries in *Spain*—
And pulled your pants off in the aeroplane.
Flick now appeared in TV panel games
Where all the players boasted household names
And took their choice of looking either Brainy
Or, if they couldn't manage Brainy, Zany.
A rarer course is just to look inscrutable.
Flick did that. Her Success was irrefutable.
She never guessed the answer even once
But no one dreamed of calling her a dunce.
They talked about her talent for repose,
Her singing stillness like a frozen rose,
Her Wisdom—unexpressed and yet supernal—
Ineffably attuned to the Eternal.

The Spring became the Summer, which in turn
Became the Autumn, you'll be stunned to learn.
The Winter gathered over *Pimlico*
And through the shadows fell the whirling snow—
It fluttered past the *Highrise* precipices
And soothed the cobbled Mews with loving kisses.
When *Flick* stepped from a taxi late at night
Her black fur hat and coat were flecked with white:
Her shoulders were alight with silver rust,
Her cuffs and collar gleamed with crystal dust.
But recently the Winters grow too mild
For *London* snow to linger plumply piled:
By noon next day the streets were full of slush,
Through which a pink *Rolls-Royce* rushed with a gush.
A famous figure skipped down *Flick*'s front stairway
Sure-footed as *Jack Nicklaus* on the fairway.
The colour of a home-made caramel,
A kid-gloved index finger pushed *Flick*'s bell.
Flick stumbled to her door still in a daze
To hear a Breakthrough forecast in a phrase.
'*Vite, vite*! *Dobbiamo* drive *comme Stirling Moss.*
Ce soir tu sei a guest of DAVID DROSS!'
La Wart helped *Flick* to dress, and with a swoosh
They pushed off in the *Rolls* to *Shepherd's Bush,*
Where soon the guards were glad to let them enter
The hallowed gates of TELEVISION CENTRE.
So horrible it stands out like a chancre,
The place looks like a wrap-round *Lubianka*—
Its curving Corridors and Zones and Areas
Recalling some sadistic plan of *Beria*'s
In which, if you run long enough, you meet yourself
And beat yourself to death and try to eat yourself.
But *Katie Wart* knew every twisted nook
And cranny of that fortress like a book.
She dragged *Flick* up a groaning escalator
Emerging in a kind of solar crater,
A cave lit like the inside of the Sun—
The Hall of Flames that men call *TC1*.
The walls were hills of countless eager faces

As tall and full as grandstands at the races.
Above were hung a hundred thousand clamps
And fixed into the clamps were blazing lamps,
While on the floor the cameras crawled and crabbed
And makeup girls adroitly poked and dabbed
At *David Dross*, who now bade them begone.
The Title Sequence rolled. The Show was on!
'Hello, good evening, fabulous, sensational,'
Dross wheedled. He seemed fully operational.
'Fantastic, super, welcome to the show,
Good evening, welcome, fabulous, hello.
Good evening ... '
For a moment *Dross* looked manic,
But lithely into shot sprang his mechanic—
Who prised a panel open in his back
And whipped-out and replaced the power-pack.
Reactivated, *Dross* resumed.
' ... Terrific.
Our topic for tonight is Scientific.
We want to probe the Nature of SUCCESS
And formulate an educated guess
At what makes some Successful People tick.
And here's one now, *Flick Fark*. Good evening, *Flick*.'
'Good evening, *David*,'
Flick said in the pause
That followed fifteen minutes of applause.
'Fantastic, super, wonderful to see you.'
Sang *Dross*,
'But tell us what it's like to *be* you.
Could you, I mean, could you, I mean, just now,
I mean, just briefly, briefly tell us how
It feels to be Successful as an actress?'
'For that I have to thank my benefactress,
Miss *Katie Wart*,'
said *Flick* with coy decorum.
The crowd roared like a riot in the *Forum*.
'Fantastic! What amazing self-effacement!'
Dross grovelled in the dust of self-abasement.
'And what will be your next amazing role?'

C

Dross probed,
　　　　　　　　'I mean, could you, what is your Goal?'
'It all lies in the lap of Destiny.
I just don't know,'
　　　　　　　　　　said *Flick*,
　　　　　　　　　　　　　　　　'We'll have to see.'
'And speaking about what the Future brings,
Here's PATRICK LOON!'
　　　　　　　　　　　wailed *Dross*, and from the wings
The *B.B.C*'s best-loved Mad Scientist
Lurched on like a gorilla round the twist.
'You say you've come from *Jupiter*,'
　　　　　　　　　　　　　　　　　　Dross quavered,
'How was your trip?'
　　　　　　　　　　　Loon faced the lens and slavered:
'Well *David*, yes. Yes *David*, yes. I've been there,
And many scientific things I've seen there.
I'm glad you asked me that. Yes yes indeed ... '
And on he gabbled as if ripped on Speed,
While *David* introduced his next sensation,
GREER GARSTLEIGH, Queen of Women's
　　　　　　　　　　　　　　　　　　　　　Liberation!
She towered nine feet seven in her clogs.
Her clogs were carved by *Dayaks* out of logs.

Her hair was something scalped from *Tiny Tim*.
Her hat had bobbing corks around the brim.
Her highly coloured language I've toned down
By 'blipping' words upon which you might frown.
'Well (BLIP) me dead. It's good to see yer, mate!'
Drawled *Garstleigh,*
'(BLIP)ing sorry to be late.
I only just flew in from (BLIP)ing *Rome.*
That (BLIP) the *Pope* was throwing an At Home.
It sounded like a love scene from a Western:
I had to talk to (BLIP)ing *Charlton Heston.*
But anyway, (BLIP) that!'
She crossed her thighs:
'And who's the (BLIP)ing bitch with the blue eyes?'
Dross told her while the screen with flares and flickers
Absorbed the fact that *Garstleigh* wore no knickers.
'Oh YOU'RE *Flick Fark*!'
shrieked *Garstleigh,*
'I'm impressed!
But help me put my (BLIP)ing mind at rest.
Just tell me how you get your (BLIP)ing rocks off.
I bet you (BLIP)ing tease their (BLIP)ing cocks off.'
'Fantastic, super, wonderful, tremendous,'
Dross drivelled,
'Welcome, fabulous, stupendous.
And now all you at home are judge and jury
As once again we welcome *Yuri Spuri,*
The guru who'll attempt to bend a spoon
While closely scrutinized by *Patrick Loon*—
And here's the lass whose spoon might soon be bent.
It's *Pauline Plank* from *Cretinthorpe,* in *Kent.*'
As *Yuri Spuri* went into his act
The screen was filling up till it was packed.
Celebrities came pouring on in streams—
The fabled faces of *Flick*'s fondest dreams.
Here came the tasteful writer *Jolly Molly,*
Her hair cerise, her cleavage full of holly.
Beside her strode her rival *Jilly Silly,*
And shrilly they swapped gossip willy-nilly.

And *Eric More* and *Ernie Less* ran in
And did their bit to swell the welling din:
Their guest was '*Jelly*' *Belly*, jaunty jazz-man,
The raunchy, roly-poly razz-ma-tazz man,
Who sang a song and sniffed a strange white powder,
Looked blank, and sang the same song even louder.
And MICHAEL LIKEABLE and RUSSELL HUSTLE
Came rushing on with that important bustle
So long associated with those two
Exponents of the Gormless Interview.
They both sat down to Interview each other
And then they Interviewed each other's mother.
'I read some clippings just before the Show,'
Said *Michael*,
'and it seems you used to know

My father fairly well. Is that true, Mum?'
And here he writhed as if his bum was numb.
'That isn't *your* Mum,'
Russell piped,
'It's mine!'
But through the fuss drilled *Dross*'s high-pitched whine:
'Amazing, super, welcome, unbelievable,
Tremendous, great, fantastic, inconceivable.
Liz, Richard, Princess Grace, Maria, Ari,
Ted, Harold, Billie-Jean, Rod, Glenda, Larry:
Success, Success, Success ... '
Blue smoke arose
From *Dross*'s ears and whistled from his nose.
One eye popped out and dangled on a wire
And from the socket leapt a tongue of fire.
Depressed mechanics clustered all about him.
Too big to stop, the Show went on without him.

Flick found herself surrounded by the Jet Set,
The Just-how-rich-and-famous-can-you-get Set.
They pumped her hand and kissed her peachy cheek
And hugged and pummelled her till she was weak.
She finally discovered with a shock
That *Yuri Spuri*'s foot was up her frock,
But hadn't thought of how she might protest
Before her chin was pressed against the chest
Of someone purring like a giant panda:
HUGE WELSHMAN, *B.B.C.* Supreme Commander!
'Miss *Fark*, a marvellous evening, is it not?
Wuff wuff. Woof woof. Warf warf. Eh eh? What what?
My life-long friend, wuff wuff, and singing star
DICK JIGGLE has admired you from afar.
For far too long, what what? Warf warf? Eh eh?
Flick, *Dick*; *Dick*, *Flick*. Well *Dick*, what do you say?'
As *Flick Fark* turned to greet this great musician
Her azure eyes grew round with recognition.
She found it hard to quell a nervous giggle,
So fearsome were the features of *Dick Jiggle*.
Dick Jiggle's hulking mouth was wet with drool,
A half-inflated children's swimming-pool
Extending three feet wide below his nose.
It also seemed to *Flick* a length of hose
(Or some long nozzle like a petrol bowser's)
Was prominent inside his satin trousers.
Dick Jiggle's Band was called the *Bleeding Gits*.
Dick Jiggle was its voice:
'Yer go' *grea'* tits.
Cough up yer number, swee'ar', 'n' I'll call yer.
Tonigh' I'm giggin', uvverwise I'd ball yer.'
Our darling would have passed out with disgust,
But then a man whose bearing won her trust
Cracked *Jiggle* with a silver-headed cane
Across the bone that might contain his brain.
'Let's mind our manners, nit-wit. Now my dear—
My name's RUSS KENNEL.'
Flick felt faint with fear.
She faced the bravest ever Film Director,

Beside whom *Hector* looked like a defector.
Russ Kennel was a synonym for Boldness:
His shamelessness exposed the age's Coldness.
Compared to *Kennel*, *Bunuel* was baloney,
Antonioni trite, *Fellini* phoney.
But why should so committed an *auteur*,
Flick wondered, want to meet a girl like her?
'The script of my next film is all prepared,'
Said *Kennel*,

'It's so fearless that I'm scared.
The title? "WOLFGANG". Subject? *Mozart*'s Life.
Young *Dick* is *Mozart*. *You* are *Mozart*'s wife.'
'Oh dear,'

sighed *Flick*,

'I don't know if I ought.'
'*Mais certainement* you ought!'

cried *Katie Wart*.

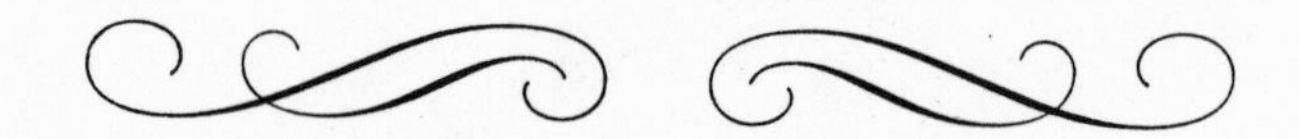

BOOK SEVEN

ACROSS the year that '*Wolfgang*' took to shoot
To draw a set of drapes would be astute.
It held the usual quota of frustrations
Attendant on *Russ Kennel*'s lucubrations,
But lacking space for giving you the low-down
On every crisis, trauma, brawl and show-down,
I'm bound to ask, alas, that you restrict your
Attention to one point—the finished picture.
The première was held in *Leicester Square*
And absolutely *everyone* was there.
I won't enumerate the personalities:
So many of them came there were fatalities,
And who did what that evening and who with
Has long ago become the stuff of myth.
They say *Marc Bolan* sat with *Ethel Merman*
And *Bolan* wore chinchilla, *Merman* ermine.
They say *Carl Foreman* sat with *Roger Corman*.
They say that *Martin Bormann* was the doorman.
There isn't any end to what they say.
The one thing certain—*no one stayed away*.
The place looked like the Mines of *Solomon*
Combined with *Guy Fawkes* Night in *Babylon*.
La Wart was *Flick*'s companion. The two ladies
Arrived in *Katie*'s midnight-blue *Mercedes*
Whose emerald piston-rings swept umpteen litres:
To park the thing you had to use three meters.
They took their places in the Royal Box—
Twin diamond-studded clouds of silver fox.
The best-dressed person in the place, however,
Was BERNARD BEAVER: also the most clever.
For *Bernie* is the wonder-boy of *Fleet Street*:
His wits are quick, his tiny feet are neat feet.
Of stature small, in height of brow immense,

He wears a pair of horn-rims like *Clark Kent*'s—
But doubtless would regard with utter loathing
The thought of using phone-booths to change clothing.
From *Savile Row* his suits come in three pieces:
They slice his valet's fingers with their creases.
Pomaded, pampered, jewelled and watch-fob sized,
The *Fourth Estate*'s great past epitomized,
Young *Bernie* is *Defoe, Shaw, Hazlitt, Swift*
And *Burke* all caught together in a lift.

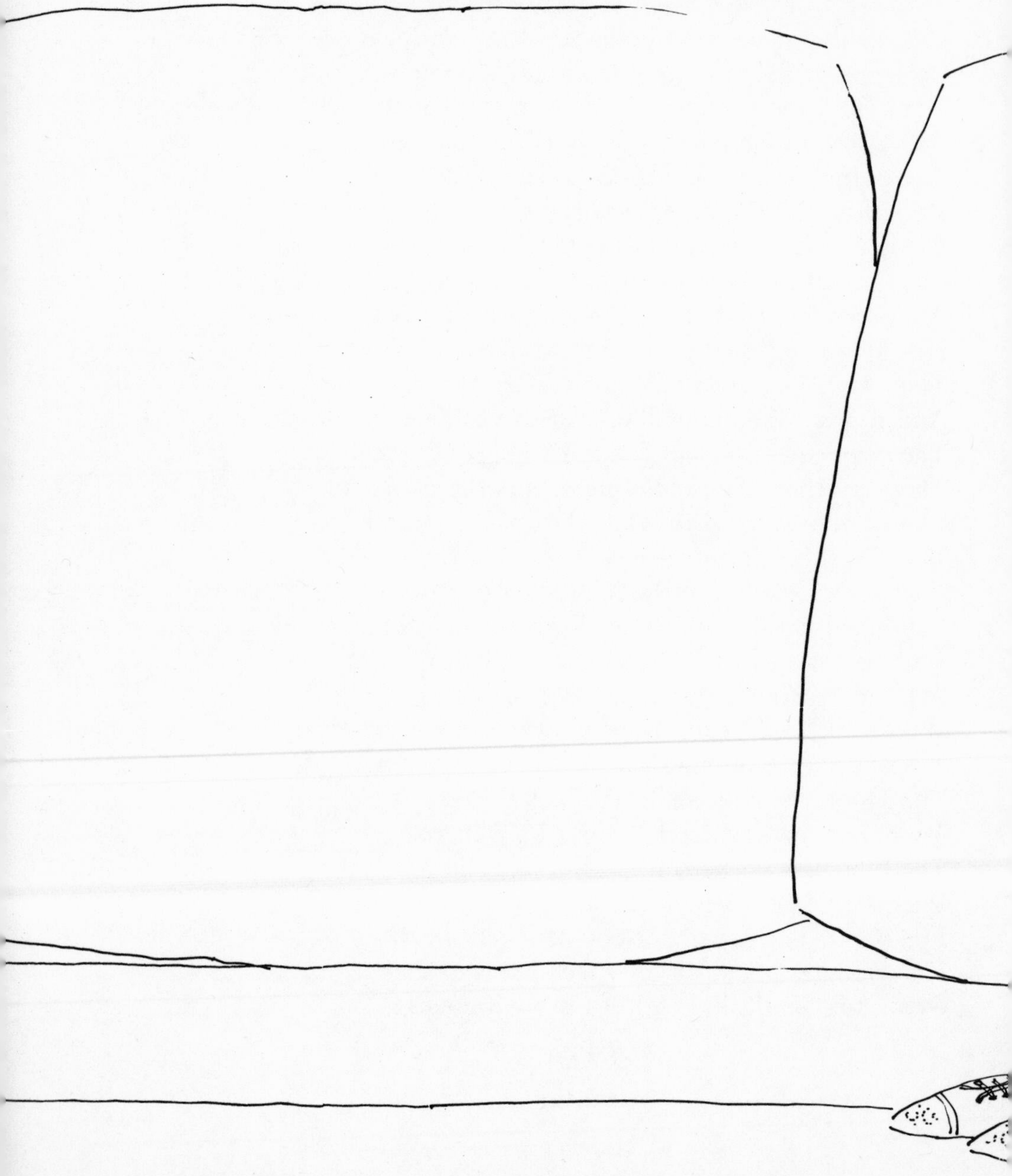

As *London*-looking as the old *Old Bailey*;
As brushed as *Brummell*, dapper as *Disraeli*;
A long Tradition's final distillation,
He stands tall at the peak of his Vocation –
The star turn of the journalistic genus,
Big cheese, bee's knees, ant's pants and peacock's penis.
But *Bernie*'s brain has one besetting vice:
A Pretty Face converts it to fried rice.
If *Kiri te Kanawa* did a jingle
For *Tampax* and released it as a single,
He'd say its greatness made his senses teeter
And made '*Aïda*' sound like '*Rio Rita*'.
Tonight he'd come to pillory a mockery
And pelt it with bad fruit and broken crockery,
But when the lights went down he got excited –
And this is what, in darkness, he indited.
'I'm at the very start bound to confess
That little else but agonized distress
Was what I felt prepared to undergo
While taking in at, as it were, a blow
The vivid Mr *Kennel*'s earthy vision
Of *Mozart*'s limpid, crystalline Precision.'
The prose of *Bernard Beaver* is *Gibbonian*,
Gymnastic, *Euphuistic*, *Ciceronian*.
His paragraphs most often aim at levity
By means of lengthiness instead of brevity.
Parentheses and clauses coil and wander
And slide around you like an anaconda.
'The script, by *Harold Half-Pint*, raises doubts,
Since silences come spouting out in gouts
Too shorn of grist for the most seasoned tongue –
And all the tongues available are young,
So young! And, it appears, so unpropitious:
As *Haydn* it was surely injudicious
To seek the services of *Tommy Steele*,
And less wise still, one cannot help but feel,
To look for *Mozart*'s lyricist *da Ponte*
By dressing up the pugilist *John Conteh*.
As *Colloredo*, *Mozart*'s persecutor,

Cliff Richard must be (must he not?) too neuter,
Too bland no matter how hard he might strive.
And *Mozart*'s children are the *Jackson Five*.'
B. Beaver's standard ploy, as you've just seen,
Is first to say how Wrong he *might* have been.
The second phase is when he Sees the Light
And very soon becomes completely Right—
Whereat he beats his breast with mock repentances,
While uttering long penitential Sentences.
'The casting of the title role, supremely,
Unsettled me—depressed me most extremely—
For surely every gesture of *Dick Jiggle*'s
Must jar like *Ronald Biggs* portraying *Biggles*;
But even (or above all) *his* endeavours
Are shaped—and here my final heart-string severs—
By one (and in that "one" what Multiplicity!)
Fair happy soul—fair happy Name!—*Felicity*.
I hope she will not mind I so address her:
I wish that I were worthy to assess her.'
But *Bernie* didn't mean those last few words:
His diffidence is *strictly* for the birds.
'*Costanze*, *Mozart*'s wife and his tormentor,
As played by Miss *Fark* holds the picture's centre.
She does not sing, she rarely speaks, she *is*—
And Warmth is hers as Genius is his.
By day she is the Artist's Inspiration
Who opens up new vistas of sensation—
Audacities of wanton intercession
Which drive him to the heights of self-expression.
This emphasis is bold, indeed unheard-of,
Yet one which I would not have missed a word of.'
When *Beaver* blows his mind over a skirt
You have to duck the shrapnel or get hurt.
'How shocking, and yet, somehow, how placating,
That *Mozart*, while engaged in copulating
With *Schubert* (finely played by *Billy Fury*)
And flagellating *Chopin* (*Yuri Spuri*),
Should shudder as his naked temptress licks
The crosspiece off a chocolate crucifix!

It is a phrase as warm as it is stark
That Mr *Jiggle* whispers to Miss *Fark*:
"No bullshi', baby, *you're* the chick for me:
I fink I'll go and write *K. Four Five Free.*" '
Here *Beaver*'s style threw off the seventh veil,
Picked up a trumpet and began to wail.
'By daylight in *Vienna* poor but buoyant,
At night the troubled *Mozart* is clairvoyant—
He hears the future *Germany* implicit
In what he writes and knows his Art illicit;
He dreams of being beaten up in alleys,
In Concentration Camps, at *Party* Rallies;
The general in command of the *SS*
Turns out to be (it is not hard to guess)
None other than his Light of Love, *Costanze*,
Who runs him over with a Mk IV *Panzer*
And does a goose-step jig on his remains
(While laughing at the stains that were his brains)
To themes excerpted from "*The Magic Flute*":
And Miss *Fark*'s foot looks brilliant in a boot.
"Wake up, wake up, my *Wolfgang*,"

she exhorts

As drops of blood drip down her leather shorts.
He wakes to kiss her nightgown's dainty hem,
Then rushes off to write his "*Requiem*"—
But Evil has forestalled the praise of *God*:
Some *Nazi* thugs (the German "*Knockout*" Squad)
With *Wagner* (*Alice Cooper*) at their head
Come back through time to fill him full of lead.
"Is this,"

he croaks,

"the end of *Wolfgang*?"

Yes.

The last shot is a lingering caress
That shows how Love and Art must come to this:
Miss *Fark* and *Hitler* (*Gary Glitter*) kiss.
The lights go up at last, and there you are—
To hail a Great New Cinematic Star.'
At this point *Bernie* blatantly let loose

D

A love-call like the cry of the Bull Moose.
'Supposing that Miss *Fark* should touch my cheek,
I swear I should not wash it for a week.
Supposing that Miss *Fark* should kick my rear
I swear I should not wash it for a year.
Supposing ... '

But a sudden lack of sound
Had caused him to desist and look around.
He was alone. He climbed down from his seat
And scampered through the foyer to the street.
He taxied off toward the *Barbican*
To join the First Night Party. What a man!

BOOK EIGHT

THE epoch-making '*Wolfgang*' First Night Thrash
Was thrown in the exotic rooftop stash
Of PETER BALLS, Theatre's Uncrowned Prince—
The evening's been a legend ever since.
The *Barbican* swarms up toward the Heavens
From Platforms all at sixes and at sevens—
Its windy Walkways hithering and thithering,
Its lonely plots of garden bravely withering.
The governing Conception is Confusion
Exalted to the level of Illusion,
A Shape-of-Things-to-Come that couldn't wait—
Too much too soon, too little and too late.
But up where *Balls* hangs out, the life is sweeter.
There's oodles more *dolcezza* in the *vita*.
His penthouse is a slice of Instant Karma,
And bigger than the *Charterhouse* of *Parma*.
The sheep-skin floor shuts out the world beneath.
The fancy drinks anaesthetize your teeth.
You gaze through walls of glass in proud elation
For miles across the brilliant conurbation
And everything you see looks hunky-dory—
There's no one there to tell a different story.
The people who turned up that night to meet
Flick Fark were the élite of the élite.
They'd all met one another long before
Which made them want to meet her even more.
While *Balls*, attired in apron and chef's hat,
Was busy barbecueing this and that,
Attentive *Katie* did the introductions—
But first she gave her charge discreet instructions.
'*Ce soir, carina, ogni* Star on Earth
Is mad to meet you. Think *von* what that's worth:
Artisti grandi begging you to do things.

But now, *je pense,* you should do *mucho* few things.
Let *klugheit* reign. Improve the shining hour.
Les hommes che hanno Talent may lack Power.'
The International Set milled all around,
All Beautiful, and all of them renowned.
The Celebrated bored the Celebrated
With old familiar scandal while they waited
To greet the new addition to their ranks:
They talked about their nest-eggs in *Swiss* Banks
And filled the air with well-connected malice.
Chief Clerk stood talking to *Maria Callas,*
Who'd recently been heard, when feeling mellow,
To sing the '*Willow*' solo from '*Otello*'
While gazing at a piece of *Aristotle*
Onassis she kept with her in a bottle.
But now *Chief Clerk* urbanely turned to *Flick*
With manners that made *Chopin* look a hick.
'Ah, what could be more pleasant,'
purred *Chief Clerk,*
'Than closely contemplating fair Miss *Fark*?
My dear, the sweet proportions of your head
Remind me of what *Berenson* once said—
That *Raphael* is the Classic of our Yearning.
Of lovely things there is no end to learning.'
The herd of supplicants in the vicinity
Concurred in thus assessing *Flick*'s Divinity,
But other words of love were soon to follow
So heartfelt they would make *Chief Clerk*'s sound
hollow,
For now there gravitated to *Flick*'s chair
The Poet Laureate, *Lord Teddybear.*
A silence fell. Uncertain and short-sighted,
He fumbled, focused, fizzed, and then ignited.

* * *

'Tonight all hail young *Flick,* whose eyes celestial
Arouse solicitude in the most bestial.
All hail her well-developed upper arms
That crush us uncomplaining 'gainst her charms.
Felicitous and sturdy village steeple!
And moss-grown at her feet lie we her people.

'Tonight all hail young *Flick* with gestures votive:
Our last and dearest branch-line locomotive.
All hail her taut and vibrant racket-strings
While envying her lucky underthings!
Felicitous and scrumptious toasted tea-cake!
I'd like to know why no one's giving *me* cake.

'All hail the frou-frou of her farthingale!
Flick Fark, farouche fritillary, all hail!'

* * *

Applause, and then the brouhaha revived,
And still the well-known worshippers arrived
At *Flick Fark*'s pretty feet to offer praise,
Though few possessed the Poet's gift of phrase.
For instance, here came large

LORD ARNOLD FATMAN,

A mandarin inscrutable as *Batman*,
Pronouncing Words of Wisdom in a mumble
That might have been a duodenal rumble.
'But let me just say this much, if I may—
I think there *is* just *one* thing I should say—
I'm very pleased to meet you here tonight:
I'd like to say just that much, if I might.
And if I may, I'd just like to say this ... '
And so the blubber brought forth ambergris.
Around they came and on and on they went:
Lord Butchfield talked to *André Prevalent*,

And there was *Perry Prykke* with *Anna Pest*,
And *Mary Quim* was promising *George Best*
His urine would do well as a cosmetic
For making trendy males smell more athletic.
(She'd done the same with *David Hockney*'s semen
But those who bought it weren't exactly he-men.)
And over there the singularly sinister
Sir Geoffrey Ripoff, wetly smiling Minister
Responsible for guarding the Environment
(The very kind of fool-factotum *Byron* meant
When calling *Castlereagh* a vulgar eunuch),
Looked pleased as *Chamberlain* just back from *Munich*
To hear *Sir Basil Spendthrift*, Architect
(With stars and ribbons heavily bedecked),
Requesting leave to build a *Top Rank* Sauna
By moving *Fingal's Cave* to *Hyde Park Corner*.
Sir Geoffrey gave his full permission willingly—
Uncovering his foul dentition chillingly.
And there were *Marvin Grabb* and *Bumphrey Quarius*,
Eclectic impresarios of various
Attempts mellifluous as warm molasses
To educate the clueless Viewing Masses—
And even now they both were hard at work
Persuading *Balls*'s rival PETER BERK
To let them screen his soon-forthcoming version
Of *Gœthe*'s '*Faust*' translated into *Persian*.
'The actors,'
ranted *Berk*,
'wear quilts for kilts.
The audience stands in a lake on stilts.
The play will run for forty days and nights
And use a natural set—the *Golan Heights*.
About the cast I'll have to tell you later—
But yes, I'll want *Flick Fark* for *Margarete*.'
All wanted her, all courted her, save one—
And here dejection counterpoints the fun,
For someone sits unmoving in a corner
As if for his own death he were a mourner.

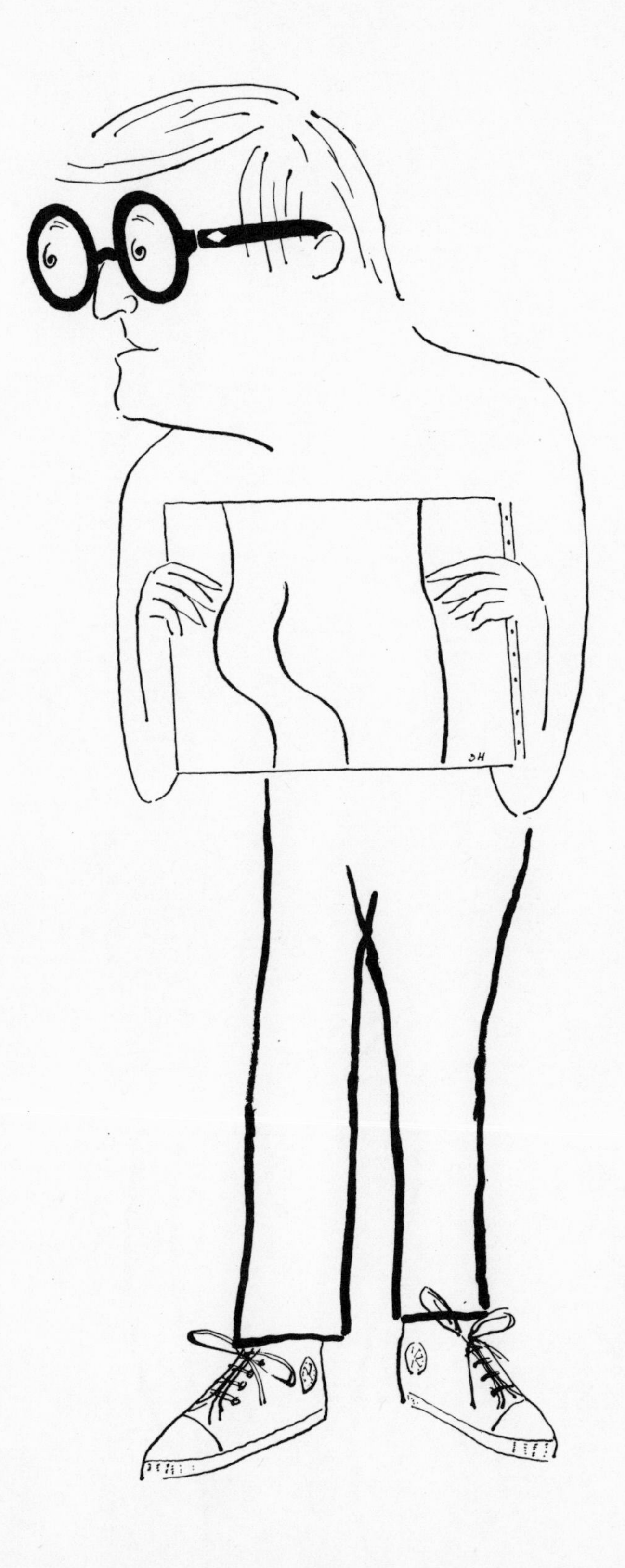

Ken Onan's face is grey-blue like a clinker
And in his lap his boneless fingers tinker
Dispassionately with his wilting quill.
He has the Gift. Alas, he lacks the Will.
The Spirit of Right Reason cries, 'Come Back,
The Dunces Reign! Return to the Attack!
Unseat triumphant Dullness from her saddle
And put the Fear of Wit in Fiddle-Faddle!'
But nothing takes his eye or primes his pen.
Most self-delighting and self-damned of men!
Since *Onan*, of all people, knows full well
The deepest hole and hottest seat in *Hell*
Are set aside specifically to cater
For him who to his Talent plays the traitor.

But that's enough of *that*. The cheery Host,
While doing nameless things to *Melba* toast,
Expressed a wish our Darling should draw near him:
Balls knew that when he spoke folk liked to hear him.
He ladled ice-cream swans full of *Beluga*
And fantasized titanic plans like *Kruger*.
He conjured up a vision of a Playhouse
To make the *Roundhouse* look like a half-way house—
A Central Drama Complex of the Nation
Ten times as big as *King's Cross* Railway Station!
'I see a hundred golden domes and walls
And grateful people call them *Balls's Halls*,'
Crooned *Balls* while soaking strawberries in
champagne—
And *Flick* was scared he might have gone insane.
'One concept will unite the whole Facility
In all Configurations—FLEXIBILITY.
For Play, for Panto, Opera, Costume Ball,
In *Balls's Halls* there'll be a hall for all.
The stages will go in and out and round
And swivel up and down without a sound—
A fluency whose actuating factor
Will be our own Plutonium Reactor.
The cost? Less than a thousand pounds a minute.
And every seat will have a toilet in it,
So nobody need leave for any reason.
We'll make the sods stay put for the whole season.'
Flick Fark and everyone in the locality
Stood dumbstruck at the man's originality.
'My *Halls* will not just leave the world agog,'
Balls boasted,
'they'll create a Dialogue,
A meeting-place to serve an Age of Doubt.
If they do not, for *God*'s sake kick me out.'
(*Balls* knew that to accomplish such a feat
Would need at least the *U.S. Seventh Fleet*.)
'The rule applies with undiminished force
That *Shakespeare* will remain our primary source.
Our Policy is clear. We mean to be

Both fresh and loyal, faithful and yet free.
"*King Lear*"s the play with which we will begin.
Which is, of course, where JONATHAN comes in.'
With difficulty *Flick* forbore to cringe
In terror at the sight of DOCTOR FRINGE.
He loomed before her like a basketballer
Who if unwound might well be even taller,
And in his bulging optics blazed unchecked
The flames of his amazing Intellect.
Imagine, if you will, the Brothers *Mayo*
Combined in partnership with *Galileo*;
Imagine, if you can, the mind of *Plato*
Combined with every *I.B.M.* in *NATO*;
Imagine, if you dare, that *Leonardo*
Wore elevator shoes like the *Mikado*:
There might be just a chance that you'd be seeing
The altogether marvellous human being
Who held *Flick*'s hand and hauled her through the
throng—
Expatiating as he loped along.
'The matriarchal structures in "*King Lear*"
Aren't really what at first sight they appear,'
Said *Dr Fringe* when nothing but the glazing
Was there before *Flick*'s eyes to stop her gazing
In wonder at the stunning midnight vista.
'It's obvious that *Gloucester* is *Lear*'s sister,
But what's less evident, although essential—
The whole foundation of the play's potential—
Is simply *Edmund* being a transvestite.'
Flick Fark stood next to *Dr Fringe* at chest-height
And strove to heed his message while her eyeline
Was ravished by the grandeur of the skyline:
The coruscating palisade of gems
That sweeps without a break beside the *Thames*
From *Chelsea* in the West East to the *Docks*—
A mountain-range of blazing tower-blocks.
'The Oedipal cathexis,'
Fringe asserted,
'*Demands* the gender-pattern be inverted.

I'm getting *Larry* to do *Goneril*,
And if *John* won't do *Regan*, *Alec* will—
With *Glenda* or *Diana* as the *Fool*.
Well, will you join us? You seem rather cool.'
Flick smiled a puzzled smile.
'I don't quite see.
If all the girls are men, then why use *me*?'
'Good *God*,'
yelped *Fringe*,
'but *you'll* be the whole thing!
That's what I'm on about. *You play the King!*'
He gestured like a crashing helicopter.
Flick started to say Yes, but something stopped her.

She knew her incarnation of this part
Could mark the dizzy apex of her Art,
And yet she heard an inner voice advise
That Destiny dictated otherwise.
She sent *Fringe* off to fetch another drink
And thereby gained some time in which to think.
Had *Katie* left? For once *Flick* was alone.
It seemed she must decide this on her own,
And in her head so many thoughts were swarming
Decisions could find little room for forming.
Her Heart, though, said her acting days were done:
She felt a whole new phase had now begun.
The larva had become the chrysalis
And now the chrysalis had come to this—
The moment of instinctive concentration
Preceding the exultant revelation,
The tremulous display of sun-shot wings.
Oh yes, she had her mind on other things—
Her solitude had formed a wall around her
That only Fate could pierce. And now Fate found her.
The flatterers outside that magic shield
Were hushed with jealousy to see it yield.
A Stranger stood beside her. Tall, thin-lipped,
Anonymous though scarcely nondescript,
He was the one and only unknown face
That *Flick* had so far seen in the whole place,
And yet she Knew. They reached out each to each.
Between these two there was no need for speech,
And though no word was spoken or bread broken
Undying Love was instantly awoken,
And *Flick* knew now she'd never play *King Lear*—
For Life was Fact, not Fiction. Life was *here*.
And so for joy our dearest Darling cried.
And so *Sir Humphrey Highrise* claimed his bride.

BOOK NINE

THE scene in which *Flick* ceased to be a spinster
Was set, by Proclamation, at *Westminster*.
The venue for her nuptials was the *Abbey*—
A solemn structure normally quite shabby,
But loud that day with fanfares and carillons
And brought ablaze by kilowatts in millions.
Flick's Wedding was a *Highrise* Enterprise:
It beggared breath. Description it defies.
It was a waking dream, a psychodrama,
A Second Coming staged in *Cinerama*,
An all-time, all-star Spectacle of Love
That *Berk* and *Balls* directed hand in glove,
With *Fringe* and *Storkins* working on the script—
While at a vast control desk in the crypt
(From which a telecast went Nationwide)
Russ Kennel sat, *Huge Welshman* at his side.
No analgesic short of acupuncture
Would help you to confront, at this late juncture,
The prospect of the Guest List read at length—
And just as you lack patience, I lack strength,
So why don't we forget the Whirlwind Finish
And simply let the dénouement *diminish*?
My Muse can no more rise to *this* occasion
Than re-create the *Normandy* Invasion:
The utmost I can do is just Suggest
And let your recollections do the rest—
For you, as I did, *saw*, in all its splendour,
The pageant that joined *Flick* to her Defender.
You know she did not flinch and would not falter
When faced with the long progress to the Altar,
But merely paused when floating through the door—
And then seemed wafted on by what she wore.

S.S. WEIDENFEL

'And here she is, and *my* this girl's got style!'
Said *B.B.C.* Reporter *David Vile.*
'And from our viewpoint high up in the Apse ... '
Said *B.B.C.* Reporter *Michael Lapse.*
' ... She still looks the most Golden Girl of all!'
Said *B.B.C.* Reporter *Stuart Gall.*
'She must 'ave took, ee-ooh, *days* to get ready!'
Said *B.B.C.* Reporter *Wearing Eddie.*
Not days. A week. Towards her bridal gown
The reckless senses ran intent to drown—
The mind had no recourse except to melt.
The dress was fashioned by *Karl Lagerfeld*
From silk-lined silk on top of silk-lined satin.
The day he finished work he burned the pattern
And blinded all the seamstresses who'd sewn it
So no one else but *Flick* could ever own it.

The way in which some hailstones are so small
You can't believe they ever fell at all,
The seeded pearls were clear and icy bright
That added white to white and light to light
And made the collar, bodice, sleeves and train
Illustrious as raindrops in the grain:
Except the outer skirt from foot to waist
Was split and turned back so the lining faced
Ahead, the hemline caught up to the wrist—
And here the silk became an analyst,
Partitioning the glare like *Newton*'s prism
Into a delicate chromatic schism
Where pools of pastel opals seemed to wander
Like waterlilies painted by *Charles Conder*.
Flick's face was hidden by a storm of veils—
Thank goodness, since by now my power fails
To reproduce the Vision Unalloyed
That clutched the elbow of *Lord Polaroid*,
Whose role it was to Give the Bride Away
(Which is, of course, the best part in the Play).
Behind them came the Bridal entourage
With *Katie Wart* decisively in charge.
She smiled a smile of mingled pain and pride
And looked almost as gorgeous as the Bride.
Her retinue of matrons and of maids
Wore everything from braids to hearing aids.
They stretched back to the doorway, and from there
Along *Whitehall*, twice round *Trafalgar Square*
And almost to the *Ritz* in *Piccadilly*.
In front came *Jolly Molly*, *Jilly Silly*,
My Lady *Freesia* and *Mary Quim*—
And after that my memory grows dim.
'Hello, fantastic, welcome!'
David Dross
Was back to show the others who was boss.
'And what we're seeing here is fascinating.
The Groom and his Best Man are gravely waiting,
And gravely now towards them like a cloud
She gravely moves through this amazing crowd.

And there's the Groom in close-up, looking brave.
He also looks appropriately Grave.
I hear he's giving her a supertanker.
For fuller news of that, here's ALAN WHANKER.'
The mouth that now chimed in wore a moustache:
Its teeth were militant, its tones were harsh.
The horn-rims poised above it were Dynamic:
The piercing view they took was Panoramic.
For *Alan Whanker* trots around the Globe
In never-ending search of things to Probe.

He claims to be on hand where grit is nittiest—
But usually shows up where girls are prettiest,
And writes a script whose lack of information
Is overlaid with lush alliteration.
'So fabulous *Flick Fark*, the fragile foundling—
The girlish, grinning, gawky, gangling groundling—
And haughty *Humphrey Highrise*—hermit head
Of huge hegemonies—are well-nigh wed.
For heritor-hidalgo-hierarch
Sir Humphrey and for fetching *Fräulein Fark*—
The pertly pouting pet of *Pimlico*—
The Countdown's over: it's "All Systems Go".'
The couple met like figures in a frieze.
They turned and sank discreetly to their knees
While *Archie Cant* went into his routine.
He wore the self-same drag to crown the *Queen*:
A family could have camped inside the cope,
The mitre would have paralysed the *Pope*.
If ever there's been more outlandish clobber
Barabbas was a priest and *Christ* a robber.
The crowd were rocked as *Archie* did his thing—
And then he asked the Best Man for the Ring.
Lord Fruitcake reached into his waistcoat pocket,
Took out a box and fumbled to unlock it.
The contents radiated luminosity
Which seemed to drain his movements of velocity
As if that multifaceted effusion
Had bruised his mighty brain like a contusion.
Lord Fruitcake in the diamond had detected
His Face a hundred thousand times reflected—
A multiple bombardment of Humility
Reducing him forthwith to immobility.
They carried him away stiff as a board
And flew him to *Morocco* to be thawed.
But meanwhile *Archie Cant* had tied the knot
While making sure the cameras got the shot.
'*Felicity* and *Humphrey*, you may kiss.
This is my final gig. I can't top this.'
By reverent fingertips the veils were raised

And on his prize *Sir Humphrey* shyly gazed.
And what have I to do now but admit
There is a time for grief, and this is it?
The distances are all so deep and wide
From which the chances race that coincide
To shape and for a moment fix in space
The breath-bereaving, death-denying Face—
The Face that leaves us rooted to the spot
(Benumbed by what it is and we are not),
Forgetting, as we view such flawless form,
Its molecules are each a whirling storm
And what connects them up must come undone:
That limpid skin is boiling like the Sun.
The poets of these last three thousand years—
The codgers and the colts, the kooks and queers—
Are linked by one delight, share one distress:
They see the holocaust in Loveliness.
To trace the outline of the holy fire
And sing the desperation of desire;
To scan the clustered atoms poised for flight
Before they scatter back into the night;
To watch the star-burst with unshielded eyes—
The lyricist does that until he dies.
It's striking, when you bring these things to mind,
That so few major bards have wound up blind.
There's *Homer, Milton* ... I suppose there's *Heine,*
Provided that you don't find *Heine* minor ...
But anyway, where was I? They embraced,
And mutually the Kiss was shaped and placed—
A gentle intermixture of bacteria
The sight of which induced wide-spread hysteria.
The music raged again without reprieve,
And as the magic couple turned to leave
The atmosphere grew stiff with Eastern smells
And purple smoke emitted by the spells
That *Yuri Spuri* cast to ward off menaces
While *Polaroid* read from the Book of *Genesis.*
With decibels that chilled you to the bone
Dick Jiggle sang '*You'll Never Walk Alone*',

A new Hit Single for the *Bleeding Gits*—
While in the font swam *Shane Gould* and *Mark Spitz*.
The song spread to the choir and congregation
And out along the ether to the Nation—
The sort of sound at which one simply chokes.
And through it all the Organ of *Jess Ffolkes*
Was roaring till his fingers were in rags:
Resplendent from the *Abbey* floor's worn flags
To where the fan-vault flaunts its *Gothic* tangle
His Instrument stood upright at an angle
Precipitous, vertiginous, funicular—
A perfect piece of *English Perpendicular*.
'And so sweet *Cinderella* plucks *Prince Charming*,'
Whined *Whanker* in tones meant to be disarming,
'And so this nubile nonesuch nereid
Who nabbed His Natty Nibs like no one did—
This nervy novice of the *nouveau riche*—
Now nimbly nets a nifty, nobby niche:
Nocturnal knick-knack for a neo-*Nero*.
Tonight they fly to *Rio de Janeiro*—
And *that* bit, I'm assured, they've *not* rehearsed.'
And off he flew himself, to get there first.

BOOK TEN

WHAT *Lady Highrise* did that night or next
Is no fit matter for the present text.
The happy pair found *Whanker* in their bed.
They kicked him out and then climbed in instead,
But how they managed later I've no clue
And wouldn't tell you even if I knew—
For Joy in Love is parcelled out unfairly
Like any other gift, and very rarely
In strict accordance with our just deserts:
A view, I think, which, even if it hurts,
Is better than supposing sensual bliss
Must be a thing the crass are bound to miss—
A psycho-physical Eleven Plus
They fail because they are not nice like us.
Such notions are attractive but mechanical,
Which makes them, when the chips are down,
tyrannical—
And though my poem has a Moral Aim
It's not as keen as *that* to place the blame.
What blame there is I first put on the Fate
That made *Flick Fark* impossible to hate:
The world could give her only adoration.
Her brain was liquefied with approbation
Until she had just Instinct left to think with—
Which barely even knows which eye to wink with.
I don't say that her impulses were mean:
They weren't that for a minute, as we've seen.
Forgive me if my logic is abrupt—
I simply call her Innocence *corrupt*.
She served to prove the point that what is flawless
Is in its essence likely to be lawless.
She had no need of tricks to help her climb:
Her inner self was climbing all the time,

And now to call her back is past our powers—
And she is *Lady Highrise of the Towers.*
She still lives on the spot where she was born,
And yet as far away as dusk from dawn.
For *Highrise House* leaves *Pimlico* behind
And soars so high you think you've lost your mind,
Until you reach the penthouse at the top.
It stands on what was once a pastry shop,
Or so, at any rate, the legend goes—
There's no one left nearby who really knows,
And *Lady Highrise* never meets the Press.
But there, if anywhere, is her address.
Up there somewhere is where she has her home
When she is not in *Paris, New York, Rome,*
At *Klosters, Courchevel, Cortina, Cannes*:
Her movements these days have a global span
And constantly around the world they wend—
Yet *Highrise House* is where they start and end.
There comes a day, blind *Homer* lets us know,
The Topless Towers of *Ilium* lie low.
Until it comes, the fortunate live high
And fool themselves, because they breathe the sky,
The atmosphere is clean down to the ground.
Their double-glazing damps the rising sound
Of people in the streets who curl up croaking—
Or else they put it down to too much smoking.
The healthy find it hard to like the sick.
And who, you ask, have *I* liked except *Flick*?
When all is said and done, is it not true
That I myself have fallen for her too?
A question that compels a pause for thought
And doomed appeals towards a higher court,
Since many a young poet picked from birth
To speak out for the Wretched of the Earth
Has found when Earth acclaims him as a speaker
His interest in the Wretched growing weaker.
He thereupon revises his aesthetic
And claims the Arts are bound to be hermetic—
By which he means he finds it far less stressful

To simply settle back and be successful.
Are Talent, Wealth and Beauty triple tyrants,
Forever tied in tripartite alliance?
Are men condemned to live and die by Luck
And loathe it only when it runs amok?
Is Fortune always to be so propitiated?
Why can't we fight it? How was it initiated?
These bones of philosophical contention
Will last as long as Time is a dimension.
From slowly spooling stereo cassettes
Directly patched into their neural nets,
Our dreaming children locked in cold cocoons
Will hear such questions like remembered tunes.
That catechistic litany will keep
Their minds alert in Cryogenic Sleep—
Conundrums they can endlessly unravel
To help them kill the light-years as they travel.
But back to Earth. It's time to call it quits
And let soft pillows soothe my cudgelled wits.
That she was Dangerous without Duplicity
Is really the whole point about *Felicity*,
Which could mean even angels are a risk—
So if you meet one, give it a quick frisk.

You've just seen a Russ Kennel *Presentation*
For Central Drama Complex of the Nation.
The art direction was by Berk *and* Balls.
Interiors were shot at Balls's Halls.
For 'David Dross' *our thanks to* 'Dr Who'.
For Patrick Loon *our thanks to* Whipsnade Zoo.
Lord Fruitcake *supplied samples of pornography*
And Yuri Spuri *did the trick photography.*
Dick Jiggle *wrote and sang* 'Yer Got Great Tits'.
The backing tracks were by the Bleeding Gits.
Lord Polaroid *is now in* 'Roll on Sex'
And 'Son of Roll on Sex Meets Madame X'
By Stanley Storkins *at the* Open Space—
And Magicote *created Miss* Wart's *face.*
Miss Fark's *gowns were by* Mary Quim *and* 'Chloe'.
Miss Garstleigh's *bra was lent by* David Bowie.
This poem was a Highrise *Enterprise.*

No wonder it was all a pack of lies.